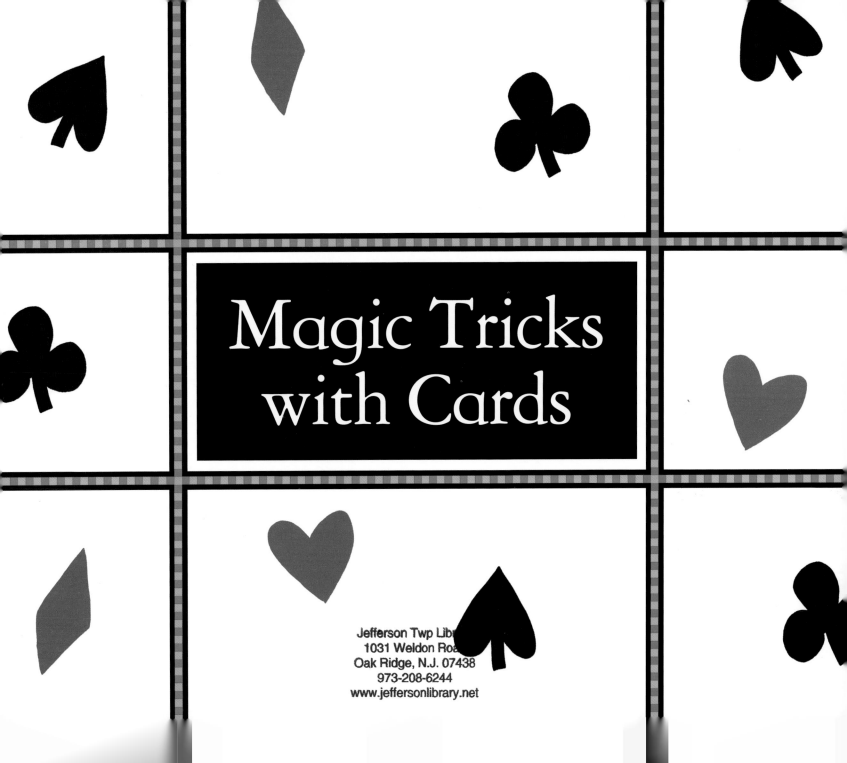

Magic Tricks
with Cards

The Child's World

Published by The Child's World®
1980 Lookout Drive • Mankato, MN 56003-1705
800-599-READ • www.childsworld.com

Acknowledgments
The Child's World®: Mary Berendes, Publishing Director
Red Line Editorial: Editorial direction and production
The Design Lab: Design

Photographs ©: Aaron Amat/Shutterstock Images, 4

ISBN: 978-1623235574
LCCN: 2013931439

Printed in the United States of America
Mankato, MN
July, 2013
PA02176

ABOUT THE AUTHOR

Jenna Lee Gleisner is an editor and author of children's books. In her free time, she loves to read, spend time with family, and take her dog for runs around the lake.

ABOUT THE ILLUSTRATOR

Kelsey Oseid is an illustrator and graphic designer from Minneapolis, Minnesota. When she's not drawing, she likes to do craft projects, bake cookies, go on walks, and play with her two cats, Jamie and Fiona. You can find her work at www.kelseyoseid.com.

Table of Contents

Fun with Cards	**4**
Shuffle It!	**6**
Card Drop	**8**
Jack and Queen	**10**
Color-Coded Card	**12**
Call the Card	**14**
Joker Slide	**16**
Card Balance	**18**
Glossary	22
Learn More	23
Index	24

Fun with Cards

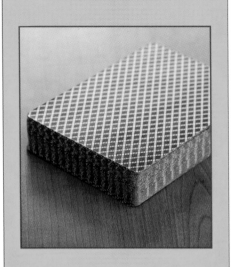

PICK YOUR DECK
Decks come in many different sizes, patterns, and colors. Choose a special deck to make your tricks your own!

Have you ever watched a **magician** do a card trick? You probably wondered how the magician did it. Card tricks can be very simple to do. This book will teach you how. Keep a deck of cards handy. Then you can show off your tricks at any time!

Before you get started, you need to learn what is in your deck. A deck of playing cards has 52 cards. They are separated into four groups. These groups are called **suits**. Hearts, diamonds, spades, and clubs are the four suits in a deck of cards. Hearts and diamonds are red. Clubs and spades are black. Each suit has an ace, numbers two through ten, a jack, a queen, and a king card. Every deck also has two joker cards.

For the card tricks in this book, you will need these things:

- Deck of cards
- Hat
- Table
- Glue stick
- Plastic cup

TRICK TIP
Always practice your trick before you perform it. Ask a parent to watch you. Or practice by yourself in front of a mirror. Then you will be ready to show an **audience** your skills.

Shuffle It!

Before you begin, there are some skills every magician must have.

First you need to learn how to fan out the deck. Hold the deck in both hands. Spread the cards out to look like a fan.

Then you need to know how to cut the deck. This means dividing the deck into two neat piles.

Finally you must learn how to shuffle the deck. When you shuffle, you will mix up the cards so they are in a different order.

STEP 1

1 First cut the deck into two fairly even piles.

STEP 3

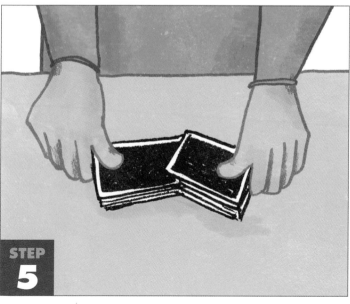

STEP 5

2 Then grab each pile the long way in each hand. Each thumb should be on one end of a pile. Your last three fingers should be on the other end.

3 Now use your pointer fingers to bend each pile slightly inward.

4 Slowly let the cards fall down from your thumbs. The cards from each pile will land in between one another.

5 Now push the cards back into one neat pile.

You just shuffled the deck! Practice, practice, practice. Soon you will be able to shuffle the cards even faster.

Card Drop

Tricks are meant to fool your audience. Learn this easy card trick to get started as a magician.

STEP
2

1 Place a hat upside down on the floor. Tell your friend you can drop more cards into the hat than she can.

2 Ask your friend to stand next to the hat. Hand her ten cards. Now tell her she must hold her arm out straight. Then she can

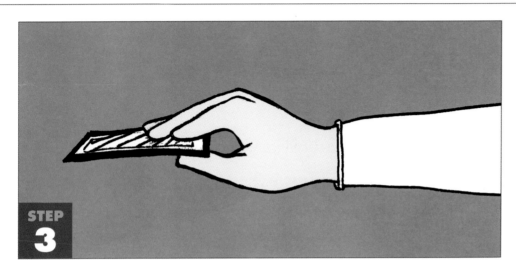

drop each card from that height. Most of her cards will miss the hat.

3 Now it's your turn. Stand the same way your friend did. But hold each card flat between your thumb and other fingers.

4 Now just drop the cards. They should fall straight down into the hat!

Jack and Queen

This trick tells a story and tricks your audience at the same time. Before you perform, move the jack of hearts and the queen of spades so they are **facedown** on top of the deck.

WHAT YOU'LL NEED:
- Deck of cards
- Table

TRICK TIP
A good magician talks to his or her audience. Telling jokes or stories makes the performance more fun for your audience. Talking is also a good way to **distract** your audience. Instead of focusing on a card's suit or number, they will focus on your story.

STEP 1

1 Tell your audience the jack and the queen had a fight. But you know how to make them friends again. Fan out the deck toward yourself.

STEP 2

2 Pull out the jack of *diamonds* and the queen of *clubs*.

STEP 5

STEP 6

3 Give your audience a quick look at the two cards. But don't say anything about the suit.

4 Then place the two cards back in the deck. But put them in different spots. Neatly place the deck back on the table.

5 Knock lightly on the deck. Ask the jack and the queen to apologize and stand next to each other.

6 Flip the two top cards over to show the jack of hearts and queen of spades. You never mentioned the suit of the cards. The audience will think these are the same two cards you just showed them!

Color-Coded Card

Some of the most popular card tricks involve finding someone's card in the deck. Fool your audience with this easy trick. Before you begin, put all the red cards in one pile. Put all the black cards in another pile.

STEP
1

1 Place the piles facedown next to one another on the table.

STEP 2

2 Ask your friend to pick one of the piles. Fan out the pile with the cards facedown. Tell her to pick a card and remember it. Then ask her to place her card facedown anywhere in the middle of the *other* pile.

3 Shuffle that pile of cards a couple of times.

4 Now fan the deck in front. Only you should be able to see the cards.

STEP 4

Your friend's card will be a different color than the rest of the cards in the pile. Make sure you don't let her see the pile. She might figure out your trick!

WHAT YOU'LL NEED:
- Deck of cards
- Table

Call the Card

Prove that you are a true magician. Choose a friend's card again with another trick.

STEP **2**

1 Shuffle the deck of cards.

2 Tap the deck sideways on the table. Make sure all of the edges are even. Peek at the bottom card while you tap the deck. Remember the card.

STEP **3**

3 Next fan out the deck. Ask your friend to pick

a card. He should hold on to the card while he memorizes it.

4 Now cut the deck. Put the top half to the right. Ask your friend to place his card on top of the deck on your right.

5 Take the other deck. Place this deck on top of the deck your friend put his card on. Fan the full deck out toward yourself. His card will be just in front of the card you peeked at!

Joker Slide

Now it's time to let a friend magically find a card in the deck. Your friends will want to see this trick over and over again!

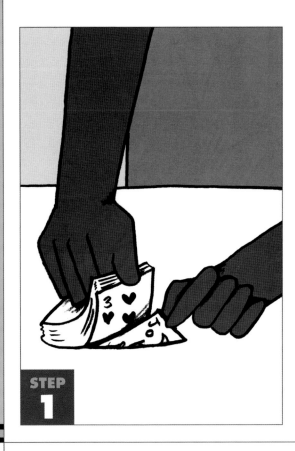

STEP 1

1 Every deck of cards has two jokers. But you need only one for this trick. Take one joker out of the deck. Place the other joker on the bottom of the deck. But don't let your friend see you do this!

STEP 2

2 Hold the deck facedown in one hand. Use your middle and ring fingers to slide down the joker in the deck. It should be farther back from the other cards.

STEP 3

3 Ask your friend to find the joker by picking a number. Let's pretend she says five. Flip up each card from the bottom of the deck. Count as you go. But keep the joker in place. When you get to the fifth card, flip up the joker.

Try the trick again. But this time have your friend pick a different number. She will be right again!

Card Balance

This next trick will really amaze your friends. They will watch you balance a cup on a single card!

STEP
1

1 Put glue on one half of one card. Spread it from one edge to the middle of the card.

STEP 2

2 Stick the card with glue to the back of the other card. Let the glue dry.

3 Then fold the side without glue back a few times. It should easily make a "T" shape.

STEP 3

4 Now for the trick! Tell your friends that you can balance a cup on top of just one card.

5 Stand the card up so the short edge rests on the table. Secretly fold out the half of the back card.

6   Now just place the plastic cup on top.

Your friends will never know how you did it!

MAKE IT A SHOW!
Learning card tricks can take a lot of practice. But soon you'll be ready to put on a magic show. Wear a cape or a hat. Invite your family and friends to watch. Sometimes your tricks won't go the way you planned. If something goes wrong, pretend it was part of your **act**. And remember, magicians never reveal their secrets!

Glossary

act (AKT): An act is part of a show. A card trick can be an exciting part of a magic act.

audience (AW-dee-uhns): An audience is the group of people who watch your tricks. Practice your tricks before showing them to an audience.

distract (di-STRAKT): You distract people when you pull their attention away from something. It is important to distract your audience so no one sees how you do a magic trick.

facedown (FASE-doun): A card with the side with the symbol turned down is facedown. You must keep cards facedown for many card tricks.

magician (muh-JISH-uhn): A magician is a person who performs magic tricks. True magicians never reveal their secrets.

suits (SOOTZ): Suits are the sets or groups playing cards are divided into. Diamonds and clubs are two suits of cards.

Learn More

Books

Bull, Jane. *The Magic Book*. New York: DK Publishing, 2002.

Eldin, Peter. *How to Be a Magician*. North Mankato, MN: Stargazer Books, 2007.

Web Sites

Visit our Web site for links about magic tricks with cards: *childsworld.com/links*

Note to Parents, Teachers, and Librarians: We routinely verify our Web links to make sure they are safe and active sites. So encourage your readers to check them out!

Index

act, 21
adult help, 5
audience, 5, 8, 10–11, 12

capes, 21
cutting the deck, 6, 15

decks, 4–5, 6–7, 8, 10–11,
    12–13, 14–15, 16–17, 18
distractions, 10

fanning the deck, 6, 10, 13,
    14–15

glue stick, 5, 18–19

hats, 5, 8–9, 21

jacks, 5, 10–11
jokers, 5, 16–17
jokes, 10

kings, 5

magic shows, 5, 21
magicians, 4, 6, 8, 10, 14,
    21
memorizing, 15

plastic cup, 5, 18, 20–21
practice, 5, 7, 21

queens, 5, 10–11

shuffling the deck, 6–7, 13,
    14
stories, 10
suits, 5, 10–11
supplies, 5, 6, 8, 10, 12, 14,
    16, 18